STEFANIA BELLONI

D0521379

JERASH

THE HERITAGE OF PAST CULTURES

Published and printed by

NARNI - TERNI

Distributed by

 Jordan Distribution Agency Co. Ltd.

AMMAN - JORDAN

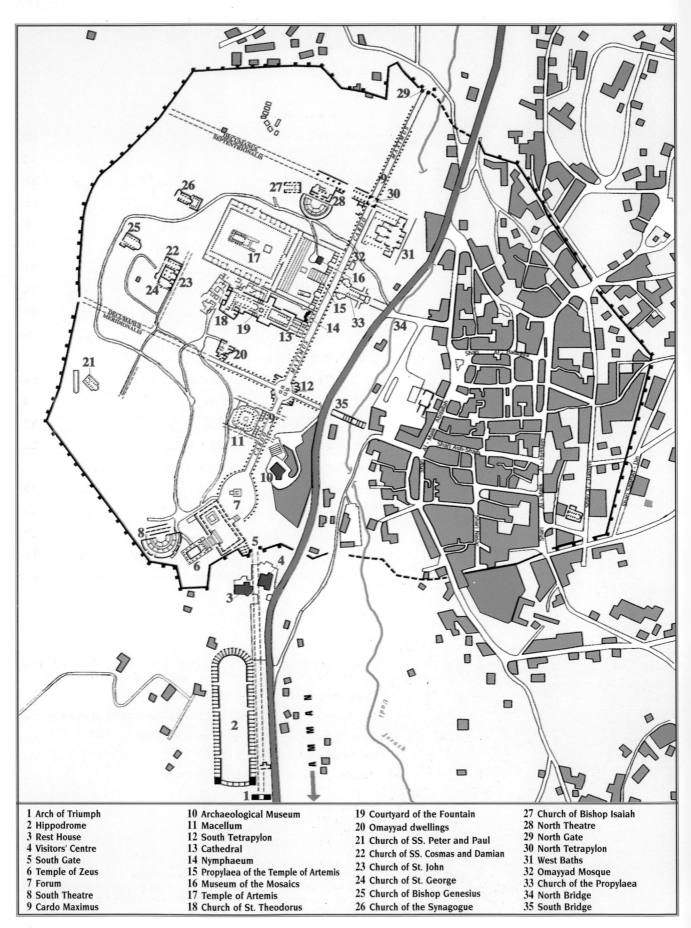

1 Arch of Triumph	10 Archaeological Museum	19 Courtyard of the Fountain	27 Church of Bishop Isaiah
2 Hippodrome	11 Macellum	20 Omayyad dwellings	28 North Theatre
3 Rest House	12 South Tetrapylon	21 Church of SS. Peter and Paul	29 North Gate
4 Visitors' Centre	13 Cathedral	22 Church of SS. Cosmas and Damian	30 North Tetrapylon
5 South Gate	14 Nymphaeum	23 Church of St. John	31 West Baths
6 Temple of Zeus	15 Propylaea of the Temple of Artemis	24 Church of St. George	32 Omayyad Mosque
7 Forum	16 Museum of the Mosaics	25 Church of Bishop Genesius	33 Church of the Propylaea
8 South Theatre	17 Temple of Artemis	26 Church of the Synagogue	34 North Bridge
9 Cardo Maximus	18 Church of St. Theodorus		35 South Bridge

Translation: **Clare Donovan**

Photos by:

Pier Giorgio Sclarandis - cov. 1st - Pag.: 1-5-10-11-16-17-18-19-21-23-27-29-31-33-34-35-36-37-38-39-42-43-51-52-53-54-55-56-57-58-59-60-64.

Paolo Pizzardi - Pag.: 4-6-12-14-20-59-60-62.

Max Mandel - cov. 4th. - Pag.: 15-22-24-25-26-30-32-35-40-41-47-48-49-63.

Palumbo/Dagherrotipo - Pag.: 3-8-9-28-46-49-50-61.

Studio Laura Ronchi - Pag.: 44-45

Archivio Plurigraf - Pag.: 7-13-20-43-58-63

Distributed by:
Jordan Distribution Agency Co. Ltd.
P. O. Box 375 - Amman - Jordan
Tel. 630191/2 - Fax 635152

Introduction

Abandonment and oblivion can often turn out to the advantage of archaeologists: it means they are able to find evidence, which is virtually intact, of those ancient civilizations which have remained immune from the ravages of time precisely because they have been long forgotten.

Jerash is one such case, a city which for centuries lay buried beneath the sand responsible for preserving its charm and impressive splendour unimpaired.

Imagine if you will, in those lands which now belong to Jordan, a fertile valley criss-crossed by numerous streams and by a bountiful river, the Chrysorrhoas, the river of gold. A place with a temperate climate and situated at an altitude of about 500 metres above sea level, in a perfect position to control the territory lying below.

A convenient stopover point for all the caravans which would have been making their way from Petra towards Syria, Mesopotamia and the Mediterranean.

Now imagine that the Romans, when they came to conquer this area in 64 A.D., under Pompey, were looking for a place to establish themselves so that they might keep control over that part of the Province which later was to become the Province of Arabia.

The combination of these two factors led to the birth of Jerash, known to the Romans as Gerasa, a city which enjoyed great prosperity during the 1st and 2nd centuries A.D., under the rule of the emperors Trajan and Hadrian.

However, it was not the Romans who first discovered this site: traces of settlements in this area actually date back to the Bronze and Iron Ages.

Subsequently, the Greeks also established themselves here, but it was only after the Roman conquest that a city in the true sense began to flourish, embellished by splendid buildings, thanks in part to the donations of the Romans who decided to reside here, many of whom were rich merchants: the names of some of them which are sculpted on the stonework of the buildings bear witness to this. The latter derived particular benefit from the *pax romana* and from the administrative autonomy which Jerash enjoyed. Furthermore, the emperor Trajan, having numbered the Petra of the Nabataeans to his conquests, brought further advantages to Jerash as a result of the new trade route, the Via Nova Traiana, which linked the two cities on the caravan route and promoted all types of exchange, whether cultural, commercial or religious in nature.

Enclosed within Roman walls, Jerash is a typical example of a Roman provincial city, centred around the *Cardo Maximus* and two parallel *decumani*: an elliptical forum, two temples, dedicated to Artemis and to Zeus, two hot baths, theatres, fountains, colonnaded streets, arcades and even a hippodrome.

As you walk among the ruins of the

ancient city you can almost feel you are experiencing once again the ancient splendours of Jerash. You can all but hear the enthusiasm of the audience crowded into the South Theatre, and can feel yourself shrouded in the silent sacredness surrounding the temple of Artemis.

As you near the Forum, the oval marketplace in which all the commercial and social activities of the townspeople took place, you can still hear a distant echo of bygone days: the buzz of voices bargaining, the cries of shopkeepers praising their wares, the shouts of children at play, the orator pleading his cause.....

Why then, after the splendour it once knew, was this city abandoned, to the extent of being almost forgotten?

The start of its decline came about with the fall of the Roman Empire and with the first invasions of the Sassanid Persians towards the end of the 3rd century.

Later on, in the Byzantine era, Jerash underwent a revival.

During that period the city was a diocesan centre; several of the temples from Roman times were modified and new basilicas and Christian churches were built using the materials of Roman buildings which had been damaged in the numerous earthquakes.

With the Persian invasion in 614 A.D., the inexorable decline of Jerash began in earnest: later it was to be conquered by the Arabs, but the recurrent earthquakes led to its inevitable abandonment.

During the Crusades in the 12th century, its temples were transformed into fortresses, but the city was destined to be completely abandoned in the 13th century.

In 1878 the Circassians established a colony here and founded the community which still continues to live in the modern part of the city.

HADRIAN'S TRIUMPHAL ARCH

Built in 129 A.D. on the occasion of the visit of the Emperor Hadrian, the splendid arch with its three fornices provides a magnificent entrance to the city of Jerash.

The **Triumphal Arch** of ochre-coloured stone stands imposingly outside the city walls: it was probably thought that the city would grow a good deal more, though in fact, with the passing of time, it remained fairly circumscribed, as can be seen by the perimeter of the boundary wall which is still visible.

The simple, yet at the same time majestic, structure of the monument, consists of a larger central arch, flanked by two smaller entrances on either side.

The semi-columns which support the three passageways rest on square pedestals. The bases of the former are ornamented with acanthus leaves, a traditional Roman decorative feature.

The two niches above the two smaller arches used to contain statues, though these are now missing.

Hadrian's Triumphal Arch.

Triumphal Arch - Detail of the central arch.

THE HIPPODROME

Presumably dating back to between the 1st and the 3rd centuries A.D., the **Hippodrome** could hold up to 15,000 people. Situated just outside the boundary wall, it is without doubt the largest building on the entire archaeological site of Jerash; it does in fact measure 245 metres in length and 51 metres in width. Remains of stables for horses and camels have been brought to light by recent excavations, but presumably the complex was intended to accommodate other types of sporting events as well. Beneath the steps which are visible on the long sides of the building, several rooms probably used as storehouses and workshops can be distinguished.

In any case, the research carried out so far has not yet established for sure whether the hippodrome was ever used or whether building works were ever completed.

It cannot be ruled out that, over the years, this vast area was used to accommodate the caravans which arrived, providing them with a place to stay and a market before they entered the city.

Around the Hippodrome's massive walls, several **tombs dug out of the rock** can be made out: these are the ruins of a cemetery from the Roman-Byzantine era, where the remains of notables and the better-off citizens were laid to rest.

*The outer walls of the **Hippodrome** at **Jerash** and in the background **Hadrian's Arch**.*

A further view of the imposing walls of the Hippodrome.

The South Gate - The main access to the ancient city was through the South Gate, coming from Amman. It was built in the 1st century A.D. closely following the same style as the Triumphal Arch dedicated to Hadrian. In fact it has three apertures and there are the same acanthus leaf decorations at the base of the semi-columns.

The South Gate - Detail of the acanthus leaf decoration.

THE CITY WALLS

The *city walls* were originally built after the middle of the 1st century A.D., but as the city developed, were extended several times.

The remaining boundary wall, around three and a half kilometres long and three metres thick, encompasses almost one square kilometre of the city.

THE TEMPLE OF ZEUS

On the high ground to the left of the South Gate, stand the ruins of the **Temple of Zeus**.

It is difficult to date this monument with any precision, since excavations have brought to light remains of several buildings from various ages.

The first building in chronological order must have been a Greek temple, dedicated to the most important pagan divinity. Later on the remains of a Roman temple were found, dating back to the middle of the 1st century A.D. The few elements now visible almost certainly date back to the period between 161 and 166 A.D.

The structure of the building, which today we can only guess at, was based on the model of a classical Roman peripteral temple. It rested on a high podium and was reached by means of a flight of stairs.

The view of the temple from below must certainly have been impressive, since the Corinthian columns which surrounded it were 15 metres high.

The huge blocks of stone visible within the area of the temple, were at one time part of the city walls and bear witness to the violence of the earthquakes which in the 8th and 9th centuries seriously damaged most of the town buildings.

Temple of Zeus.

Temple of Zeus - Remains of the outer wall.

The Temple of Zeus

Temple of Zeus - One of the decorative niches.

The Temple of Zeus seen from the South Theatre.

THE SOUTH THEATRE

The largest and best conserved of the three Roman theatres in Jerash is the **South Theatre**, a magnificent building which stands on a rise near the temple of Zeus. Built in the reign of Domitian (1st century A.D.), the monumental complex could hold more than 3,000 people. There are thirty-two rows of seats, many of which are still marked with Greek numbers. The stage is divided on two levels and is elegantly decorated with niches and aedicules, as well as by soaring columns mounted on pedestals.

The utmost attention was paid to every detail of its architectural conception: for example, the theatre was oriented on a north-west axis, to make sure that the sun would annoy the spectators as little as possible. Furthermore, the exceptional quality of the acoustics and the careful restoration carried out mean that today it still provides an ideal venue for cultural events, such as those which the International Festival of Jerash hosts every summer.

The South Theatre.

The elegant pink limestone and white stone stage in the South Theatre.

Greek inscriptions and decorations on the raised step of the stage.

The South Theatre - Detail of the steps.

THE FORUM

The **Forum** in Jerash, the large oval marketplace, the heart of the city's social and political life, is one of the most interesting archaeological finds on this site.

This complex, like all the most important urban structures essential to a large city in the Roman Empire, was built towards the middle of the 1st century A.D.

Elliptical in shape, the square is still surrounded by the original 56 Ionic columns, surmounted by an uninterrupted line of tripartite architraves. To the north the colonnade opens onto the Main Road, the *Cardo Maximus*, with a series of Corinthian columns.

Its out-of-town position (it does in fact stand at the end of the Cardo Maximus) was presumably due to the fact that not only did it need to accommodate traditional mercantile and administrative activities, but would also have been used for cultural and religious events, connected with the nearby Temple of Zeus.

The paving of the forum, which measures ninety metres by eighty, is in an excellent state of preservation. The outer area consists of wide limestone slabs, which get gradually smaller as they reach the centre, where we find the remains of a podium on which originally a statue would have stood.

Later on the statue was removed and a fountain or water pipe installed in its place, the plumbing of which is still visible below the paving near the podium.

A column now stands on the podium surmounted by a metal frieze on which every year, on the occasion of the Festival of Jerash, a torch is lit as a symbol of the themes of art and culture which are central to the Festival.

The Forum, seen from the South Theatre.

The paved floor of the Forum surrounded by the Corinthian columns which bordered the oval marketplace.

A *general view* of the Forum, with the podium at the centre. A column with a metal frieze currently stands upon it.

The Cardo Maximus - south side.

THE CARDO MAXIMUS

The colonnaded street was a characteristic feature of imperial Roman cities, and is fairly widespread in all the Asian provinces. It would seem that its origin lies in the Hellenized East, where spectacular and monumental architecture was an important aspect of town planning.

The **Cardo Maximus** is the main thoroughfare of the city of Jerash. It extends for about 800 metres from south-west to north-east, that is from the Forum to the North Gate, and was marked out between 39 and 67 A.D.

It was flanked by Ionic columns, some of which were subsequently replaced with Corinthian columns in the second half of the 2nd century. Around five hundred of them are still standing.

Most of the city's buildings and a large number of shops, with entrances between the colonnaded arcades, gave onto the Cardo Maximus, which is paved with limestone blocks. The road was later embellished with fountains, the most important of which was the one dedicated to the nymphs (Nymphaeum).

The Cardo, also known as the Colonnaded Street, was intersected by two **decumani**, to north and south, which formed two crossroads, each one marked by a *tetrapylon*, a four-fronted arch.

At the crossroads of the Cardo with the *south decumanus*, the **South Tetrapylon** can be distinguished, a particularly monumental structure. It stands at the centre of a square (*tetrakionon*) bordered by ruined buildings at its four corners. It consists of the remains of four square pilasters, surrounded by niches, each one of which is surmounted by columns which supported the four-fronted arch.

The **North Tetrapylon**, which marks the intersection of the Cardo with the *North decumanus*, dates back to the 2nd century. Tastefully conceived and embellished with fountains, it consisted of four arches supporting a dome.

Detail of the **C**orinthian columns which flank the **C**ardo.

The Cardo Maximus

The paving of the Cardo Maximus.

On this page and on the following: *The tetrapylons at the crossroads of the Cardo with the decumani.*

A further stretch of the columned street of the Cardo.

The Macellum - On the left of the Cardo Maximus as you proceed north, is the Macellum, the meat market. It consists of a large space bordered by columns and characterized by the composite central tank, the upper part of which has been lost.

35

THE CATHEDRAL

The Cardo gives access, via a staircase, to the place where at one time the **Temple of Dionysus** stood, built in the 2nd century A.D.

The material of the original building was later used to build the city's **Cathedral**, in the second half of the 4th century, at the exact spot where the Temple used to stand.

Unfortunately, little remains of this latter construction of the Byzantine period. The stairs in front of the church are an adaptation to the Byzantine building of the temple staircase standing in front of the podium.

Its basilican structure consisted of three naves with an apse shut off by an iconostasis. The magnificent portal is finely decorated and gives some idea of the majesty of this holy edifice.

Behind the cathedral is the **Church of St. Theodore**, (late 5th century), which, together with the cathedral, formed part of a larger sacred area utilized in the Byzantine epoch. This too was a basilica with three naves, the remains of whose elaborate mosaics have been preserved.

Behind the church of St. Theodore is the so-called **Courtyard of the Fountain**, where the remains of a square basin can still be seen. Originally, the courtyard atrium was used each year by the faithful as a meeting and commemoration place in memory of the miracle of the Marriage of Cana.

The Cathedral - main entrance.

Some examples of marble decorations in the Cathedral.

One of the Cathedral entrances.

The entrance to the Church of St. Theodore.

THE NYMPHAEUM

In front of the Cathedral building, in a partial state of preservation, lies the beautiful fountain dedicated to the water nymphs: the **Nymphaeum**.

It is a splendid example of an ornamental fountain from the late 2nd century A.D.

The Nymphaeum, about twenty metres wide and originally fronted by a portico, is bordered by a concave wall adorned with two orders of niches. Here are the statues from which the water used to pour out. This water would then gush out from a basin surrounded by sculptures depicting lion heads, producing a particularly spectacular effect.

The upper part of the wall was decorated with stuccos, while at the bottom it was covered with precious green marble from the Aegean.

Several finely sculpted Corinthian capitals are visible on the columns which are still standing. The whole was completed by a semi-dome in the shape of a shell, probably decorated with mosaics. The pink granite basin at the base of the fountain was added in the Byzantine era.

The Nymphaeum from the 2nd century A.D..

The Nymphaeum

The Nymphaeum - The pink granite basin added in the Byzantine epoch.

The Nymphaeum - Detail of the upper part of the concave wall, and a general view.

THE TEMPLE OF ARTEMIS

The **Temple of Artemis** (2nd century A.D.) is undoubtedly the most impressive temple building in the city, both because of its central and raised position, and also because of the importance of the divinity to whom it was dedicated, Artemis (Diana) protectress of the city.

Situated within the *témenos*, a sacred enclosure 161 metres by 120 metres in size, the temple was surrounded by walls flanked by arcades of Corinthian columns.

Below the *témenos* is the **Mosaics Museum**, where some fragments of mosaics found in the churches of Jerash are kept.

On the eastern side lies the monumental entrance to the temple, the **Propylaeum**, a vestibule of huge visual impact, a splendid proof of the Roman grandeur of the time.

The Temple itself is peripteral and is situated on a podium about four and a half metres high. The Corinthian columns of the atrium in front of the temple are very well preserved. Further on, the cella, with niches surmounted by gables, is visible: originally the whole was covered in marble and housed the statue of the Goddess.

In front of the building is an altar for sacrifices, a common feature of local temples as it is for Syrian temples too; the same goes for the holy water basins used for sacred ablutions, which are also located in the temple courtyard.

Below the central building there are underground naves which can be reached from the sides. The central nave is the longest and leads to a room in a good state of preservation, beneath the eastern area of the temple.

It is thought that this monumental complex was never finished. The excavation works have brought a constant stream of materials and finds to light, which have been of great help in piecing together the history of the temple.

In the Byzantine epoch this building was used as an artisan workshop producing crockery and kitchenware, if the furnace remains found in front of the temple are anything to go by, while later on the Arabs used it as a fortress.

The Temple of Artemis.

The Propylaeum, monumental entrance to the Temple of Artemis.

The Propylaeum.

Various views of the Temple of Artemis.

49

The Temple of Artemis

Details of the Corinthian columns of the Temple.

THREE BYZANTINE CHURCHES: SS. COSMAS AND DAMIAN, ST. JOHN THE BAPTIST AND ST. GEORGE

Ever since the archaeological site of Jerash has been the object of excavations and in-depth studies have been carried out on its remains, around eleven Byzantine churches have been brought to light, although the experts are certain that there are still more.

Some of the splendid mosaics which decorated them are still in place and visible, some have been removed and are on exhibition in the Museums of Amman and in the local Mosaics Museum, while yet others have been covered up to avoid further damage.

In the western part of the ancient city, adjacent to one another, stand the three large Byzantine churches of **SS. Cosmas and Damian, St. John the Baptist and St. George.** These date back to the first half of the 6th century and were built within a few years of one another.

Built in the reign of Justinian, they are the best preserved buildings of that epoch. They were constructed on top of previous Roman buildings and still house interesting remains of the precious mosaics which decorated their floors.

According to the custom of the time, each church could celebrate a single mass each day: the three churches were therefore built next to one another, with the aim of being able to celebrate three masses in the same day.

CHURCH OF SS. COSMAS AND DAMIAN

The most northerly church was the last to be consecrated, in 533, and has the best preserved mosaic floor in the whole city and part of the walls which surrounded it are still standing.

The church is dedicated to the twins Cosmas and Damian, two doctors who devoted themselves to the special care of the poor and the needy, who were martyred in the reign of Diocletian. The mosaics of what was the central nave depict zoomorphic figures as well as geometric decorations and symbols of the art of medicine. Furthermore, the benefactors who financed the building of the church are depicted, as well as several bishops of the city.

SS. *Cosmas and Damian*.

On this page and on the following pages: *Some of the precious mosaics which decorated the pavements of the three churches.*

CHURCH OF ST. JOHN THE BAPTIST

The central church was built in 531 under the jurisdiction of Bishop Paul.

Its simple structure terminates in an apse of an unusual horse-shoe shape. The floor mosaics which cover the main nave are unfortunately not very well preserved, but some symbolic figures are still visible, dedicated to flora and fauna and the portrayal of the Four Seasons. Furthermore, the depiction of several holy Egyptian cities, such as Alexandria and Memphis, can be distinguished.

CHURCH OF ST. GEORGE

This church was the first to be completed at the beginning of 530. With a basilican plan, of the three churches this is the one which was least damaged by the numerous earthquakes which afflicted the area at that time; there is in fact proof of its also being used after the earthquakes which occurred in the 7th and 8th centuries. Unfortunately, however, precisely because of its better state of preservation, it was subjected to greater plundering by iconoclasts. The latter irreparably damaged the mosaic designs, while the debris on top of the other two churches served to some extent as protection for the precious mosaics which decorated them.

Church of St. George.

CHURCH OF BISHOP GENESIUS

Behind the three Byzantine churches we find the remains of the Church of Bishop Genesius.

The mosaic floor is dated 611, which is why it is possible to confirm that this was the last building constructed in Jerash before the arrival of the Persians in 614.

THE SYNAGOGUE CHURCH

Behind the Temple of Artemis is the Synagogue of the 3rd or 4th century A.D., facing towards the city of Jerusalem. Later on in 531 a church was built above the Synagogue.

THE NORTH THEATRE

Not far from the Temple of Artemis, proceeding along the *north decumanus*, are the remains of the **North Theatre**, building work on which first started in the 1st century A.D. It was inaugurated in 165 A.D. to be precise, but was then extended during the 3rd century. Smaller than the South Theatre, it is not as well preserved as the former. Initially used as an auditorium for the reading of poems or staging of plays, the building was covered and presumably was also used as a meeting place for the townspeople, on the occasion of public councils and assemblies.

In the 14 rows of seats lower down, you can read interesting inscriptions in Greek, such as those which mark the *phylai*, the areas set aside for the various groups which sat there regularly when the town council was voting.

The upper seats were added later on, bringing the number of seats up to about 1,600.

The North Theatre, like the Temple of Artemis, was used subsequently as an artisan workshop for the production of pottery.

The North Theatre.

The North Theatre.

THE HOT BATHS

Level with the *North Tetrapylon* we find the remains of the town's **West Baths**. The other thermal complex, the **East Baths** lies beyond the river Wadi ed Der, the ancient Chrysorrhoas, which divides the new city from the old.

The West Baths, built in the 2nd century A.D. are the better preserved even if many features have not yet been brought to light by excavations. In any case, it is thought to be the largest thermal complex built by the Romans in the territories of present day Jordan.

The design of the baths according to Roman tradition was fully respected in Jerash as well: there was a *Frigidarium*, a *Calidarium*, a changing room and two magnificent pavilions. The large domed vault of one of the pavilions is still in a good state of preservation. Unfortunately the East Baths are less clearly visible, given their poor state of preservation, which is why it is difficult to date them with accuracy.

THE OMAYYAD MOSQUE

The **Omayyad Mosque** is the only mosque known to exist in Jerash and stands near the West Baths, a few metres from the Cardo Maximus.

Dating back to the 7th or 8th century, what remains of it only came to light during some excavations carried out in 1981.

The Mosque was built around a Roman house, abandoned maybe as a result of an earthquake. It stands in the atrium of the house surrounded by columns, and the *mirhab* has been created out of an elegant decorated niche.

THE NORTH GATE

Built in 115 A.D. under the Emperor Trajan, the North Gate was formed by a single arch. An important road led from it, which joined Jerash to Pella, another important city in the Roman Decapolis.